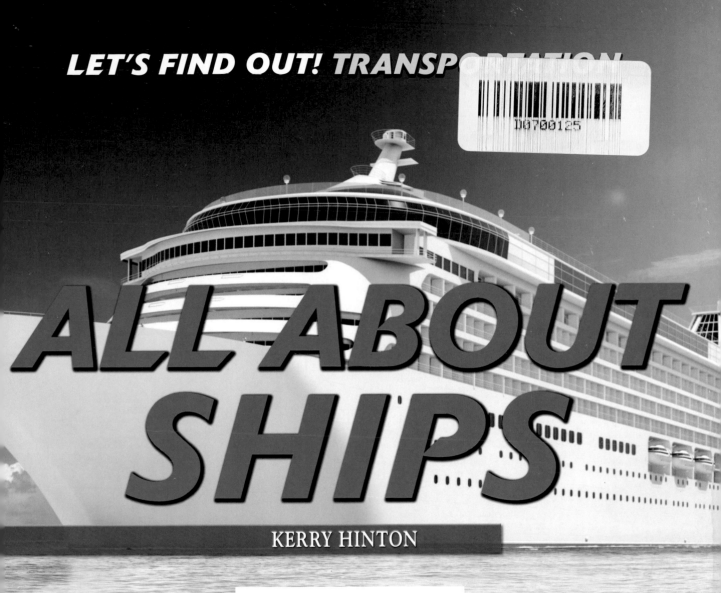

ALL ABOUT SHIPS

KERRY HINTON

Britannica®
Educational Publishing

IN ASSOCIATION WITH

ROSEN
EDUCATIONAL SERVICES

Published in 2017 by Britannica Educational Publishing (a trademark of Encyclopædia Britannica, Inc.) in association with The Rosen Publishing Group, Inc.
29 East 21st Street, New York, NY 10010

Distributed exclusively by Rosen Publishing.
To see additional Britannica Educational Publishing titles, go to rosenpublishing.com.

First Edition

Britannica Educational Publishing
J.E. Luebering: Executive Director, Core Editorial
Mary Rose McCudden: Editor, Britannica Student Encyclopedia

Rosen Publishing
Christine Poolos: Editor
Nelson Sá: Art Director
Nicole Russo: Designer
Cindy Reiman: Photography Manager
Sherri Jackson: Photo Researcher

Library of Congress Cataloging-in-Publication Data

Names: Hinton, Kerry, author.
Title: All about ships / Kerry Hinton.
Description: First edition. | New York : Britannica Educational Publishing in association with Rosen Educational Services, [2017] | Series: Let's find out! Transportation | Includes bibliographical references and index. | Audience: 1-4.
Identifiers: LCCN 2015048089| ISBN 9781680484434 (library bound : alk. paper) | ISBN 9781680484519 (pbk. : alk. paper) | ISBN 9781680484205 (6-pack : alk. paper)
Subjects: LCSH: Ships--Juvenile literature. | Shipping--Juvenile literature.
Classification: LCC VM150 .H56 2017 | DDC 623.82--dc23
LC record available at http://lccn.loc.gov/2015048089

CONTENTS

MOVING THINGS FROM HERE TO THERE

Ships carry goods that are bought, sold, and traded around the world.

Every day, people, animals, and goods are moved from place to place around the globe. This process is called transportation. Since almost 75 percent of the earth's surface is covered by water, ships do a lot of this work. Ships are large boats that can carry passengers or cargo for long distances over water.

Before the invention of the airplane, crossing oceans and large bodies of water could only be done by ship. Although there is faster transportation now, ships are as important today as they have ever been. Commercial ships move almost four billion tons of cargo every year. Food, wood, and minerals are taken from farms, forests, and mines to factories around the world. There, they are used to make millions of products ranging from anvils to zippers. These new manufactured goods are then shipped around the world.

THINK ABOUT IT

If 75 percent of Earth's surface is covered by water, how much of its surface is covered by land?

Large cargo vessels may take weeks or even months to reach their destinations.

THE PARTS OF A SHIP

Ships are carefully designed to operate safely and efficiently.

Ships are basically large boats, so they have many of the same parts. The front of a ship is called the bow. The back is the stern. A ship's left side is known as the port side. The right is the starboard side. A ship's frame, or body, is called the hull. The keel is like the ship's backbone. It keeps the ship from tipping over. A rudder is a flat panel

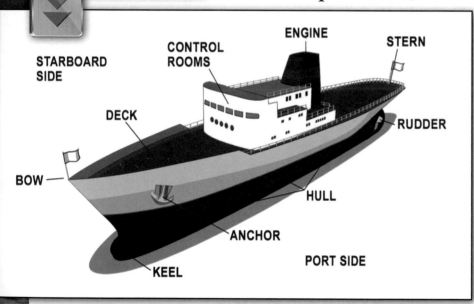

STARBOARD SIDE

CONTROL ROOMS

ENGINE

STERN

DECK

RUDDER

BOW

HULL

ANCHOR

PORT SIDE

KEEL

that is moved from side to side to provide steering control.

Ships usually have many decks. The decks are like the floors of a building. Cabins for passengers, engine and control rooms, and spaces for cargo are often on different decks. An engine inside the ship provides energy to propellers at the back of the ship. The propellers propel the ship through the water. When the ship is not moving, a heavy metal anchor may be lowered into the water. This keeps the ship from floating away.

From Yesterday To Today

The first boats were carved from trees. They were called canoes. At first, people used their hands to move their canoes through the water. Eventually, wooden oars were used instead of hands.

Later, people attached sails made of cloth to **masts** on their boats. This allowed them to use the wind to power bigger boats through the water. These bigger boats were the first ships. Using sail and oar power together allowed these ships to move faster.

Ancient artwork tells us that ships were a large part of everyday life even thousands of years ago.

> By the 1400s ship design had improved. Aside from trade, ships were also used for exploration and war.

> A **mast** is a long pole that rises from the bottom of a ship or boat and supports the sails and rigging.

By the 1400s ships began to carry as many as three masts. Christopher Columbus, Vasco da Gama, and other explorers used ships like this to reach unexplored territory. When new lands were found, settlers moved there on ships. Once travel between countries became easier, trade increased and ships became bigger.

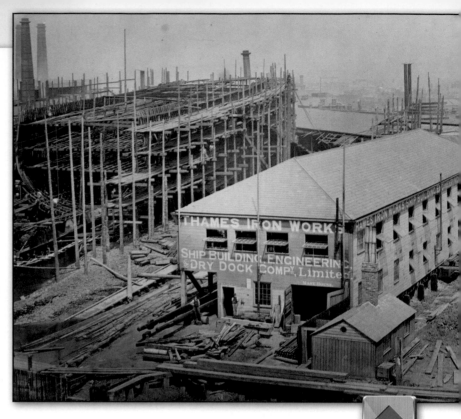

For the next four hundred years, most ships were made mainly of wood. Wood was a plentiful resource. Then, a big change came to ship design. In the 1800s iron began to replace wood as the most popular shipbuilding material. It was stronger and made it possible to build larger ships that could carry more goods.

Iron was also used to build the mighty steamboats that replaced sailing ships. The first steam engines ran on coal. The engines became smaller as time went on, leaving

Iron made it possible to build even larger ships. The skeleton of a new ship under construction can be seen above.

Ships can be powered by different fuels. Here, men shovel coal into large fires to create energy to power their ship.

more room for more cargo. These improvements had an important effect on trade around the world.

Thanks to modern engines, a ship can now cross an ocean in a few days instead of a few weeks. Oil powers most modern ship engines today, but some use coal or nuclear energy.

THINK ABOUT IT

Why are engines more reliable than sails for powering a ship?

CARGO SHIPS

The first cargo ships were built by ancient Egyptians. They carried trading cargo as well as huge pieces of stone. The stones were used to construct buildings and monuments. Today, cargo ships carry much more.

Cargo ships carry almost anything that can fit in boxes, crates, bales, and barrels. They also carry products that are hard to ship in containers, such as coal, grain, steel, lumber, and farm products. Some cargo ships can even carry small numbers of people.

There are several types of cargo ships.

Before the steam engine was invented, ancient vessels were powered by humans using oars.

Automobiles are driven onto the loading area of a roll-on/roll-off ship to be shipped overseas.

One type is known as a roll-on/roll-off ship. These ships have large ramps at the bow or stern that allow vehicles to be driven on and off cargo ships for transport. This saves hours of loading and unloading time. Two other major types of cargo ships are tankers and container ships.

THINK ABOUT IT

Some cargo ships are huge—more than 1,000 feet (305 meters) long. On a ship that big, do you think you can feel the movement of the ocean?

TANKERS

Ships called tankers transport liquids, such as oil and chemicals. The ships contain many tanks, so if one tank fails, the rest will remain safe. Tankers also carry less dangerous liquids such as orange juice and vegetable oil. Most tanks are contained in the bottom of the ship. Oil tankers carry oil, which is taken to refineries, where it is used to make gasoline, diesel fuel, and heating oil. These new products are loaded into new tankers and taken around the world.

Modern tankers can transport ten times more than ships could fifty years ago. This

Oil tankers like this one carry almost two-thirds of the world's oil supply.

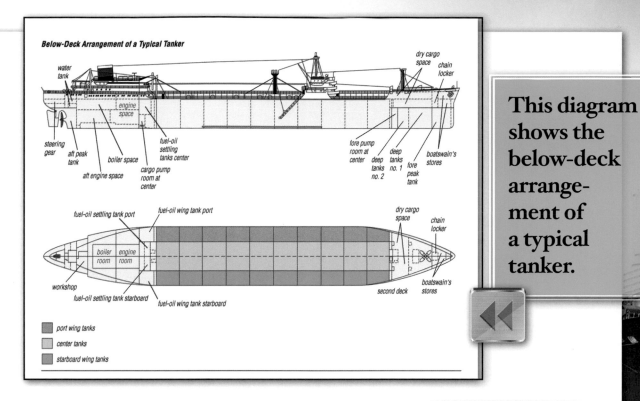

Below-Deck Arrangement of a Typical Tanker

water tank

engine space

steering gear

aft peak tank

boiler space

aft engine space

cargo pump room at center

fuel-oil settling tanks center

dry cargo space

chain locker

fore pump room at center

deep tanks no. 2

deep tanks no. 1

fore peak tank

boatswain's stores

fuel-oil settling tank port

fuel-oil wing tank port

boiler room

engine room

workshop

fuel-oil settling tank starboard

fuel-oil wing tank starboard

dry cargo space

chain locker

second deck

boatswain's stores

port wing tanks

center tanks

starboard wing tanks

This diagram shows the below-deck arrange-ment of a typical tanker.

increase in capacity means larger ships and larger risk. Any spill from a supertanker could seriously damage the environment or hurt people. Chemicals must be transported in special tanks lined with protective coatings. A tank's inside coating depends on the liquid being transported.

Capacity is the largest amount or number that can be contained in something.

CONTAINER SHIPS

Containers are large boxes made of metal. They come in two lengths, but they all have the same width so they can be stacked and transported easily. They hold goods that have been manufactured and are ready to sell. Container ships can carry food, televisions, clothing, and more. Containers are stored above deck as well as below. Megaships can carry almost twenty thousand containers.

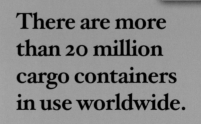

There are more than 20 million cargo containers in use worldwide.

Shippers must keep track of every container for the system to work. They do this by labelling each container and checking when it departs and arrives. Some shippers track their containers electronically. When ships pull in to port, the containers are removed by a crane. From there, they are taken to their destinations by trucks or by trains.

Heavy duty cranes are needed to move containers off of ships. An empty container can weigh as much as 6,000 pounds (2,722 kilograms).

A **crane** is a machine with a swinging arm for lifting and carrying heavy loads.

INDUSTRIAL SHIPS

Many of today's oil rigs are portable. They can be towed by large ships to new locations.

Industrial ships carry out an industrial process at sea. Some industrial ships are also factory ships. As the name suggests, these ships are like factories at sea. For instance, fish factories are ships that work out in the ocean with a fleet of large fishing boats. As ships catch fish, they pull alongside a factory ship. The factory ship processes and freezes the fish. Once loaded, it can be taken directly to shore for sale.

Some industrial ships do not go anywhere for a long time. For example, deep-sea oil rigs are placed in one spot to pump oil from the ocean floor. They have crews that work, eat, and sleep on board. Some industrial ships incinerate hazardous waste far at sea.

COMPARE AND CONTRAST

Compare an oil rig out at sea with one on land. How could they be different, if at all? Could one replace the other?

Factory ships are floating factories where fish are caught, processed, and frozen.

MILITARY SHIPS

A navy is the branch of a country's armed forces that fights on, under, or over the sea. Many countries have navies to defend themselves. There are many different types of ships that navies use. Some military ships are used to transport soldiers, sailors, and their equipment around the world.

Aircraft carriers are the largest military ships. They can carry up to one hundred aircraft that can take off and land on the ship. It takes hundreds of men and women to keep an aircraft

> Aircraft carriers cost billions of dollars per year to operate.

carrier afloat. Cruisers, destroyers, and frigates are all much smaller than aircraft carriers. They protect carriers against attack and launch missiles and torpedoes. Many navies have ships that perform a small number of jobs. Hospital ships are floating hospitals. Helicopters transport patients to and from hospital ships.

COMPARE AND CONTRAST

Airplanes take off from and land on an aircraft carrier's flight deck. How is this deck different than the deck of other types of ships?

Destroyers launch missiles to defend aircraft carriers.

21

Submarines are ships that can go underwater and stay there for months. They don't even need to come to the surface for fuel and supplies. They are nicknamed subs. They patrol the sea and can launch torpedoes during wartime. They have tanks that are filled with

Some military submarines can stay beneath the surface for months at a time.

Think About It

HMS *Artful*, a British submarine, has enough fuel and air to stay underwater for twenty-five years. Can you think of reasons why the ship would need to come up to the surface? What things might the crew need to survive?

The use of space is very important on subs. Military subs can carry about 150 sailors and the food they need to survive.

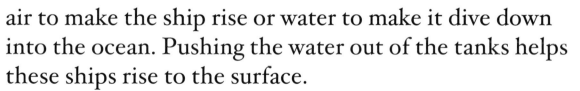

air to make the ship rise or water to make it dive down into the ocean. Pushing the water out of the tanks helps these ships rise to the surface.

Submarines are also used by scientists to explore the deepest parts of oceans. Scientific researchers and explorers usually use smaller submarines. These submarines may have mechanical arms, cameras, and other tools to help scientists study the underwater world.

Passenger Ships

Ships that carry large numbers of people are called passenger ships or ocean liners. They were very popular before airplanes made it possible to travel far distances in a short time. By the 1960s these ships could make the trip from America to England in four days.

Before air travel, passenger ships provided the only means of transportation across oceans.

Though not as common, passenger ships are still in use today. They don't travel as fast as they used to, but they use less energy than airplanes. Most trips across the Atlantic Ocean take about seven or eight days and are designed for enjoyment.

Modern ocean liners are called cruise ships, and they can be enormous. Some are almost as long as megatankers. They transport thousands of people. They have dining rooms and cabins for guests to sleep. Many cruise ships feature exercise rooms, swimming pools, shopping, and live entertainment.

THINK ABOUT IT

Since airplane travel is faster than ocean travel, why would anyone sail to their destination?

Today's cruise ships feature restaurants, theaters, and pools.

Specialty Transport

There are many other types of ships that are used to transport things. Many are used for a specific, or single, job. Cable ships lay and repair underwater cable on the ocean floor. Underwater cables are used for **telecommunication**, for electric power, or for other purposes. These ships help keep the world connected.

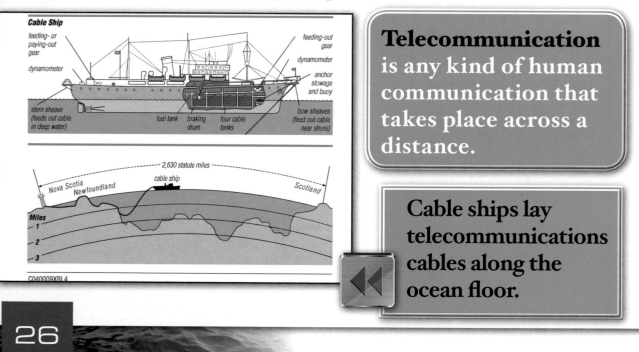

Cable Ship

feeding- or paying-out gear

dynamometer

feeding-out gear

dynamometer

anchor stowage and buoy

stern sheave (feeds out cable in deep water)

fuel tank   braking drum   four cable tanks

bow sheaves (feed out cable near shore)

2,630 statute miles

Nova Scotia Newfoundland   cable ship   Scotland

Miles
1
2
3

C040009XBL4

Telecommunication is any kind of human communication that takes place across a distance.

Cable ships lay telecommunications cables along the ocean floor.

Livestock carriers move sheep, cattle, and other animals from one place to another.

Icebreakers are ships that clear a path through frozen water for scientific ships and other vessels. Some are military ships operated by the U.S. Navy and Coast Guard. Research ships are smaller ships that carry scientists who conduct research at sea. Some research ships are used to look for oil. Some allow scientists to study sea creatures in their environment. Research ships often have laboratories on board.

The hulls of icebreaking ships have an extra layer of steel to aid in breaking through frozen waters.

THE FUTURE OF SHIPPING

The world's merchant **fleet** is huge. It includes more than eighty-five thousand ships of all sorts and moves the majority of freight around the world. Nine out of every ten pounds of goods on our planet are transported by ship. Since

A **fleet** is a group of ships or vehicles that move together or are under one management.

As the population of the world increases, more ships will be built to carry more goods to more people.

Egypt's Suez Canal enables ships to travel between Europe and Asia without going around Africa.

thousands of ships are involved, international agreements and uniform industry practices are needed to maintain an orderly flow of commerce.

Ship technology will continue to improve. The future of shipping may include ghost ships, or ships that are controlled by a captain on land. The captain will be able to navigate the ship based on data that is received from the ship's sensors. Remote-control ships are just one development that is likely to affect how goods are shipped all over the world.

GLOSSARY

anchor A device usually of metal that is attached to a boat or ship by a cable and that when thrown overboard holds the boat or ship in place.

bow The front end of a ship.

captain The officer in charge of a ship.

cargo The goods transported in a ship.

craft A small boat.

deck The floor of a ship.

freight Goods or cargo carried by ship, train, truck, or airplane.

hull The frame or body of a ship.

keel A timber or plate running lengthwise along the center of the bottom of a ship and usually sticking out from the bottom.

merchant Relating to trade. A merchant ship carries people or cargo for a fee.

oar A long pole with a broad blade at one end, used for rowing or steering a boat.

port The left side of a ship.

propeller A device consisting of a hub fitted with blades that is made to turn rapidly by an engine and is used especially for propelling airplanes and ships.

rigging The ropes and chains used aboard a ship that control the sails and supporting masts.

rudder A flat movable piece (as of wood or metal) attached to the rear of a ship or aircraft for steering.

starboard The right side of a ship or aircraft (looking forward).

stern The rear end of a boat.

submarine A vessel designed to operate underwater.

vessel A craft larger than a rowboat that is used for transportation on water.

FOR MORE INFORMATION

Books

Lavery, Brian. *Ship: The Epic Story of Maritime Adventure*. New York, NY: Dorling Kindersley, 2010.

Lynch, P. J. *The Boy Who Fell Off the Mayflower, or John Howland's Good Fortune*. Somerville, MA: Candlewick, 2015.

Mechem, Liz. *Disasters at Sea: A Visual History of Infamous Shipwrecks*. New York, NY: Skyhorse Publishing, 2014.

Potter, Jonathan. *Ships* (Look Inside Cross-Sections). New York, NY: DK Children, 1994.

Ross, David. *Visual Encyclopedia of Ships*. London, UK: Amber Books, 2013.

Spilling, Michael, ed. *Submarines 1776-1940*. Edison, NJ: Chartwell Books, 2013.

Spilling, Michael, ed. *Submarines 1940-Present*. Edison, NJ: Chartwell Books, 2013.

Websites

Because of the changing nature of Internet links, Rosen Publishing has developed an online list of websites related to the subject of this book. This site is updated regularly. Please use this link to access this list:

http://www.rosenlinks.com/LFO/ship

INDEX